The Ech

SECOND BC

C000162228

Cotswold Walks

by Christopher Knowles

Ten more walks compiled from the Lifestyle supplement of the Gloucestershire Echo.

Family strolls of between 2 and 5 miles, including refreshment stops along the way.

REARDON & SON
Cheltenham, England

INDEX

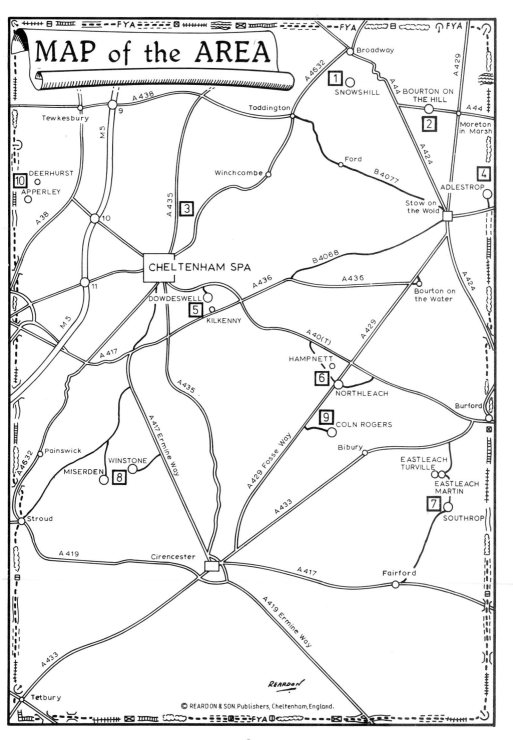

MAP of the AREA

Broadway

A4632

1 SNOWSHILL

A44 BOURTON ON THE HILL

A429

A44

Moreton in Marsh

2

Toddington

Tewkesbury

9

A438

M5

A435

Ford

B4077

A424

4

ADLESTROP

Winchcombe

3

10 DEERHURST

APPERLEY

A38

10

11

M5

Stow on the Wold

CHELTENHAM SPA

B4068

A436

A436

Bourton on the Water

A424

DOWDESWELL

5

KILKENNY

A417

A435

A40(T)

HAMPNETT

A429

6

NORTHLEACH

Burford

9 COLN ROGERS

Painswick

A4632

WINSTONE

MISERDEN

8

A417 Ermine Way

A429 Fosse Way

Bibury

EASTLEACH TURVILLE

EASTLEACH MARTIN

7

SOUTHROP

Stroud

A433

A419

Cirencester

A417

Fairford

A419 Ermine Way

A433

Tetbury

REARDON

© REARDON & SON. Publishers, Cheltenham, England.

1. Snowshill

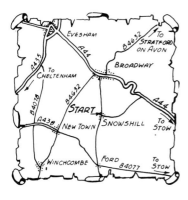

Distance: 2.5 miles

Time: 1hr 15mins continuous walking

Map: OS Pathfinder 1043 (SP03/13, Broadway and Chipping Campden)

Starting Point: Grid ref 097341

Terrain: Field and track with a little road. Some mud after rain, particularly in woodland parts. Gently undulating with a few undemanding slopes.

Refreshments: Snowshill Arms, Snowshill. Teas in the village hall in summer.

THIS is a short walk but no less enchanting for that. It follows a path around a well-known village in the Cotswolds - Snowshill - and may therefore offer the opportunity to visit one of the area's most entertaining highlights, Snowshill Manor. The walk may easily be lengthened, as a glance at the OS map will indicate. Snowshill is just south of Broadway.

There is no problem parking in Snowshill since there is a National Trust car park just to the north of the village, no more than a few yards from the first houses. Exit from the car park on to the road and turn to the right, keeping to the pavement that will lead you towards Snowshill village. On the left the fields rise up to the sky, on the right, beyond the stone wall, the land tumbles down to the valley bottom below. As you enter the village proper ignore the road that leads away and up to the left and, keeping to the main thoroughfare, descend and pass some houses of recent construction on the right. Not long after you will come, also on the right, to a much older and more picturesque house with its several sets of windows and its typical Cotswold gables and big chimney.

A row of cottages is to the left; and then you come to the green with the church ahead of you and the pub on the right. The entrance to Snowshill Manor is here too, on the right.

The history of the manor is of considerable interest. Although there are definite signs of an earlier medieval building from about 1500, the present construction dates for the most part back to the late 17th and early 18th Centuries, built in the typical Cotswold manner, of local stone with copious use of mullioned windows and gables. The garden, filled with old-fashioned roses, echoes the formality of earlier times. The original house belonged to Katherine Parr, the last wife of Henry VIII but it owes its unique character to the property's last owner, Charles Wade, who purchased it in 1919. He restored the house and, himself something of a scholar, devoted his time to the creation of an extraordinary collection of what may very loosely be termed objets d'art and curios. His money came from the family sugar business based in the West Indies. He, however, continued to lead a rather spartan existence, refusing the luxury of electric light and sleeping in a nearby cottage in a Tudor cupboard bed.

His collection is, to say the least, varied. There are Persian lamps, illuminated parchments, possibly the greatest collection of Japanese armour outside Japan, musical instruments, early means of transportation and old tools, to name but a few; and all this is in a small, pretty but unassuming, hardly cosmopolitan, Cotswold village. It is a hackneyed expression, but Mr Wade was clearly in the illustrious tradition of the English eccentric.

The walk continues in the direction of the church, which you will pass to your left. Nobody seems to have a good word (architecturally speaking) for this temple ('the church is a rebuilding, and comes as rather a shock in this beautiful hill village), but there is an interesting font and pulpit inside; and several chest-tombs with arched panels, typical of the east Cotswolds, in the churchyard.

Follow the road around as it begins to climb, passing a wall to the right that seems to have staddle-stones inserted into its fabric, and then Oat Hill Cottage on the left, with its brooding carving of a bearded head on a roof there. Then, just after Oat House, you will see a concrete track leading quite steeply down to the right. A public footpath is indicated here.

Follow this down towards the fields. There is a hedge to your right and a wooded bank to your left. Before you are rough pastures dotted with sheep and beyond more woodland sprouting from the sides of the enfolding valley.

Continue along the track until you come to a gate. Pass through and carry on at the edge of grazing land until you soon come to another gate. As you approach it you will notice a rather tropical looking pool across the fence to your right. On the gate itself it is clearly written that beyond lies private property; so you should keep to the left of it and continue on around the base of the field with fence and hedgerow on your right. On your left is a little hillock, littered with dead trees and scored with the lines created by sheep hooves.

The path climbs a little, levels out and then curves round to the bottom of a bank that you can see ahead. In the corner on the right you will come to a stile. Cross this and turn immediately left to follow a path which cuts its way up the hillside between hedge and newly planted trees. To your right there will be views across the thistles to a church tower and the vale beyond. Snowshill village is strung out along the valley behind you.

The clear path rises and falls. You will pass a gate on the right which is to be ignored, and keep to the path as it rises again and comes to an end at a stile and, to its left, a bridle gate. These will take you into a long sloping field that curves around the valley with dense woodland at its rim. The path follows the curve of the field about a third of the way up the slope and heads for a stile set into a fence about 100 yards to the left of a farm, with farmhouse of the warmest Cotswold hue, ahead of you to the right. As you approach the stile the path rises sharply and will take you onto a narrow lane.

Turn right and then, where the lane divides, take the left, rising fork and follow it as it passes above the farm. The lane develops a green ridge. Above you to the left are Littleworth Woods and to the right dappled shades of ploughed land, meadows and Snowshill village.

So, pass the converted cottages on the right and continue along this peaceful byway. A large house appears to the right on the other side of the valley; then the track will begin to rise slightly, riding the lower part of the ridge, and then enters a wooded area. Almost as soon as it does so you will see a sign for a footpath on the right. Down below to the right ahead of you is another farmhouse.

Obey the sign by crossing a kissing gate and bear a little right to follow the path at the top edge of a sloping field among some trees. The path, though obvious, is well nettled, and quite stony as it gradually descends to a corner where it bears left and brings you more fully into the field. Keep to the right hand margin of the field and continue to descend, with stubby berry-clad bushes on the right.

Soon, Broadway Tower appears ahead of you to the left. The fence on the left will come in at you a little and then eventually begin to veer away as you approach woodland ahead. Where the field meets the woods is a stile. Cross this, go straight and quickly bear right along a muddy woodland path. Again there may well be a lot of nettles hanging over the paths, though in winter they will have lost their venom.

The path descends until it meets a little wooden bridge and swing gate in a trough at the edge of the woods and the base of a hillside. Turn right and head up the slope with woodland to your right. The path is not obvious at this stage; but if you keep rightish, though cutting off an obtruding corner of the field, and head for a couple of trees that appear above you slightly left, you won't go far wrong. As you near the top of the slope - which is part of the dramatic abyss at the top of which sits Snowshill - and as a fence comes in at you from the left, you will see a wooden and stone stile on your right.

Cross this stile into another sloping field and head up diagonally to the right, towards some trees, keeping left of a modern house which will appear to the right. Soon you will come to another stile set into a fence on your right; this will take you into another meadow.

Again follow a diagonal line by the field to the left of the house until you come to another stile beneath a row of trees. Go over this on to a drive, turn left and then immediately right on to the road, which you follow for a short distance until you come to the car park on the right.

6

The SNOWSHILL Walk

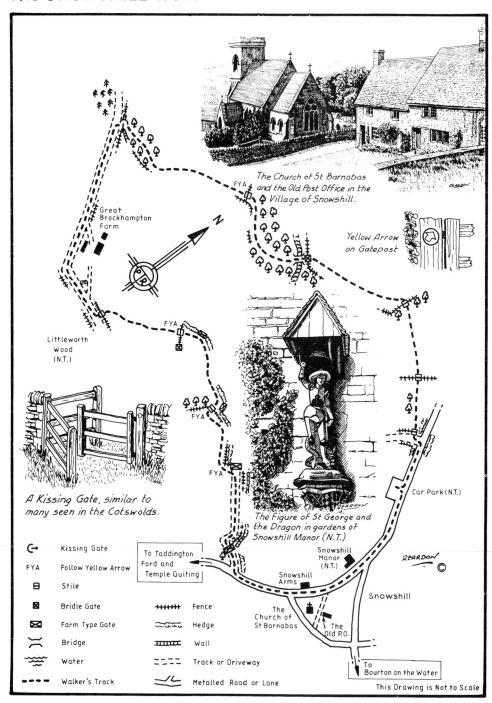

The Church of St Barnabas and the Old Post Office in the Village of Snowshill.

Yellow Arrow on Gatepost

Great Brockhampton Farm

Littleworth Wood (N.T.)

A Kissing Gate, similar to many seen in the Cotswolds.

The Figure of St George and the Dragon in gardens of Snowshill Manor (N.T.)

Car Park (N.T.)

To Taddington Ford and Temple Guiting

Snowshill Manor (N.T.)

Snowshill Arms

Snowshill

The Church of St Barnabas

The Old P.O.

REARDON ©

To Bourton on the Water

This Drawing is Not to Scale

⌇ Kissing Gate		
FYA Follow Yellow Arrow	┼┼┼┼┼	Fence
🯄 Stile	〰〰	Hedge
🯄 Bridle Gate		
⊠ Farm Type Gate	⫟⫟⫟⫟	Wall
⤡ Bridge	⹀⹀⹀	Track or Driveway
Water		
▪▪▪▪ Walker's Track	⌇	Metalled Road or Lane

7

2. Bourton on the Hill

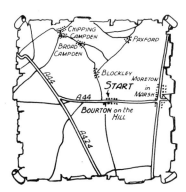

Distance: 3 miles

Time: 1hr 30mins continuous walking

Map: OS Pathfinder 1043 (SP03/13, Broadway and Chipping Campden)

Starting Point: Grid ref 176324

Terrain: Meadow and track and some lane walking. Undulations are gentle and undemanding. There may be some mud underfoot.

Refreshments: The Horse and Groom, Bourton on the Hill.

THIS walk is perfect simplicity. It is rather short, no more than an elongated stroll. But in a short space it offers much in the way of scenery, views, flora and fauna and architecture. Bourton on the Hill is on the A44, about two miles to the west of Moreton in Marsh.

Let us begin with a quotation from an old guidebook: "If Bourton-on-the-Water is the Venice of the Cotswolds, then Bourton-on-the-Hill must be the Babylon of the district, for though its cottages and its church sit quite happily and securely on the steep hillside - seeming, indeed, to be part of it - their gardens, which are the feature of Bourton, hang before them like a series of huge window-boxes. No, window-box, however, ever held such a display as gladdens the heart of the traveller whose way takes him through Bourton. Aubretia, lilies, wallflowers, roses and 101 other blossoms whose names are known universally to gardening enthusiasts fill these gardens at Bourton almost, one might think, to bursting point." Bourton-on-the-Hill (once 'on-the-Merche') is certainly an attractive village, perfectly poised above the surrounding countryside, although it lies just below the high wolds. The church, dedicated to St Lawrence, was originally Norman and some of the original, stolid pillars in local stone still stand to one side of the nave. One item of particular interest within is the Winchester bushel and peck which were early standardised weights from the reign of Elizabeth I.

Begin the walk by taking the road on the left as you enter the village from Moreton, just before the church. The road bears to the right, by a proper red telephone box, so that the church is above you on your right. On your left you will see a sign indicating a path. Take this, a track really, which runs between two stone walls and leads to a gate. Go through the gate into a field, dotted with a few trees, with a stone wall still to the right and above it a stately house. Shaggy little fields with low hedges slope away to the left, down to the plain below.

Go through another gate into a field with gentle pleats. Already the expanse of Bourton stretches out behind you. Enter another field by means of a gate, with a low hedge on the left - one of a series that looks as if they were built for a steeplechase - and trees ahead of you. As you move forward so some gleaming modern buildings will appear far away to the left, and beyond them, distant hills.

Continue across the field until you come to a wooden fence - a little way up the field, probably to your right if you have maintained the same line, you will see a stile. Cross this and head across another field towards another set of trees. Among them is a kissing gate that takes you into a grove of trees and then almost immediately another. Pass through the

8

gates into another field and head across this, too, between a pair of spinneys. At this point you will doubtless catch glimpses of the verdigris cupola of Sezincote Manor.

In fact you are already in the grounds of the Manor, that very English style of parkland which is a satisfying mixture of order and natural exuberance. Walk on, cross an estate road, head for a dead tree on its side and then proceed down a slope, covered with boxed-in saplings, towards some more trees. On your right the estate road winds its way towards the manor.

At the bottom of the slope the path passes between a tree and a wooden fence which encloses a variety of colourful trees, and then passes a gate marked 'private' on the left before slipping between a point where fences converge. The path passes between two dark and crowded little ponds to emerge into another meadow. To your left is a gleaming strip of lake; but to your right is a chunk of the Indian Raj transported to the heart of the temperate English countryside. Sezincote Manor is a startling sight indeed, with its Mogul domes and turrets, 'in the Hindu style'.

It is really a marvellous piece of English eccentricity. It dates back to the 18th century when one Sir Charles Cockerell, who made his fortune with the East India Company, had the manor built as, it is to be supposed, a sort of tribute. His brother had a hand in the design, along with architects Daniell and Repton (landscape gardener at Sezincote), and Nash. The Prince Regent, no stranger to flights of fancy, was favourably impressed during a visit in 1807, a memory that was to lead to the creation of his own Brighton Pavilion.

Follow the path across the field, pass through a gate by a water trough and enter another field that slopes upwards. Head up and a little to the right, towards the top right corner, ignoring any gates that may tempt you into the woodland near the manor. In the corner you will find stone walls and a gate.

Pass through the gate onto a road. Turn left to find fine views away to the east. As you walk down the road you can see, across to the right, the village of Longborough and its church. Then another church will appear behind that.

Pass a cottage on the left and head on down. There are open fields to the right and a low hedge giving on to a meadow dotted with a few trees. You will pass through the gateway of a wooden fence, after which the lane will begin to level out. Soon you will approach another gateway, the domain, it seems, of a fox which likes to trot nonchalantly across your path, taking a little spring air.

Then comes another gate and just before it, to the left, an expectant row of trees that line an old water course. Pass through the gate and follow the track as it bears left and then right, towards Upper Rye Farm. As you approach it you will see other farm buildings across the fields to the left, notably one with gaping arches; and behind you may catch glimpses of the dome of Sezincote Manor.

Pass the entrance to the farm on your left and head for the black barn, keeping to the right of a wooden fence. You will come to a gate - pass through and turn immediately left, heading between the barn and the farmhouse. Keep going towards another gate and cattle grid - Bourton-on-the-Hill will soon appear to the left. Once past the cattle grid, continue along the track to another one, after which you should cross the stile that you will find immediately on the left.

This takes you into a field. Follow its left hand margin, the farm with the gaping-arched barn away to the right, and a streaming ditch on your left. In the corner of the field there is a little footbridge. Cross this and bear sharp right into another field. Follow the right margin here and keep going, ignoring a tempting gate on your right. Bourton is not far in front of you but it is a measure of the skill of the masons of the past that it blends harmoniously with its surroundings and is scarcely visible.

Eventually you will come to a stile in the top right corner. Cross this onto a path that files through shrubs and trees along the edge of the stream, curls to the left and deposits you at another stile. Cross this and head across the field to another stile. Then cross a road, then another stile and continue along the edge of the field, with a low hedge to your right, until you come to a tree where you should turn right along a rough path between hedges, Bourton plainly visible above you to the left.

THE DELIGHTFUL VILLAGE OF BOURTON-ON-THE-HILL IN GLOUCESTERSHIRE.

REARDON

This path sort of splutters out at a corner. Turn left so that there is a tree and fence to the right and head toward the gate. Continue walking up the slope through a succession of fields and gates noting the fine house to the right. This is Bourton House, which dates back to the 16th century. The fine nearby tithe barn, also of that era, is marked in the name of one Richard Palmer who was linked by marriage to the Overbury family, one of whose ilk, a Sir Thomas Overbury, was infamously murdered in the Tower of London in 1613 by the slow administration of poison. He was placed there by Lady Essex because he opposed the marriage between that lady and Robert Carr, favourite of James I. He died after living in agony for months and it was only some years later that the truth emerged. The Carrs were too influential to suffer, but several 'accomplices' were hanged.

Continue until you come to the path on the right that leads up to the church. As you take this path, a stone wall is on the left - note the faded stone inscription above a little wooden doorway set into the base, which reads 'Deo Gratias AD 1919'.

The BOURTON on the HILL Walk

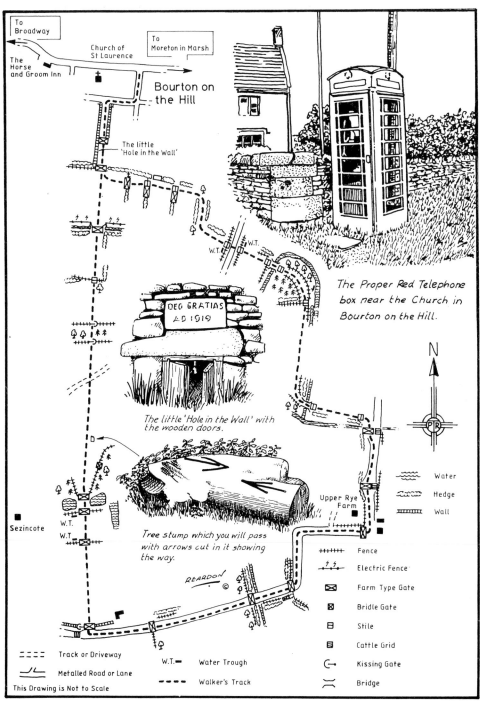

To Broadway

Church of St Laurence

To Moreton in Marsh

The Horse and Groom Inn

Bourton on the Hill

The little 'Hole in the Wall'

W.T. W.T.

DEO GRATIAS A.D 1919

The Proper Red Telephone box near the Church in Bourton on the Hill.

The little 'Hole in the Wall' with the wooden doors.

Sezincote

W.T.

W.T.

Upper Rye Farm

Tree stump which you will pass with arrows cut in it showing the way.

REARDON ©

	Water
	Hedge
	Wall
+++++++	Fence
⚡	Electric Fence
⊠	Farm Type Gate
⊠	Bridle Gate
目	Stile
目	Cattle Grid
⌐	Kissing Gate
⤼	Bridge

N

P R

- - - - Track or Driveway

Metalled Road or Lane

This Drawing is Not to Scale

W.T. ➡ Water Trough

- - - - Walker's Track

11

3. Nottingham Hill

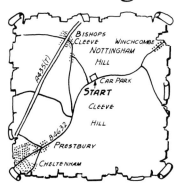

Distance: 3.25 miles

Time: 1hr 30mins continuous walking

Map: OS Pathfinder SO 82/92 (1066 Cheltenham)

Starting Point: Grid ref 985270

Terrain: Some metalled lane and pavement but for the most part grassy hill paths, woodland and tracks.

Refreshments: The High Roost pub and Cleeve Hill golf course club house.

HERE'S a walk for which we can stay in the area of Cheltenham, albeit on the other side of the town in the shadow of Cleeve Hill. Indeed Cleeve Hill will be a constant, distant companion to the walk as we discover a near neighbour, Nottingham Hill. This is not a long walk, but will involve a steady ascent, worthwhile as always for some truly spectacular views. The starting point is on the A46, four miles to the north of Cheltenham in the parking area opposite the public loos where the road passes near the summit of Cleeve Hill.

The best place to park is on the A46 in the layby opposite the public loos where the road passes near the summit of Cleeve Hill. There are one or two other parking areas in the vicinity, so park where you can. Walk along the pavement, descending the hill in the direction of Cheltenham. On your right there are fine views - in fact you are looking across Stockwell Common at a height of 728 feet towards the Severn Vale, with Bishop's Cleeve at the foot of the hill (hence the name, cleeve being another way of saying cliff), the Malvern Hills and the Forest of Dean. Beyond, 45 miles away, are the Welsh Mountains.

Walk down on the pavement until, very soon, you come to Stockwell Lane on the right, just before a bus stop and a proper red telephone box. Turn right there and proceed downwards.

This narrow, metalled lane is bounded by dense bushy, hedgerow on either side, although it soon opens up to the right. Then a path - in fact a drive - will appear to the right which you ignore; the road will descend still further to pass white cottages on the left, and more drives and trees to the left and right. The lane plunges ever more steeply through a close wrapping of foliage to pass more cottages and to then open up to the Severn Vale before you in the distance.

After a while the lane will begin to level out, as it passes Post Office Lane on the left. Shortly after, opposite a cottage on the left by the name of Innisfree, with its garage with green doors, is a stile on the right. Go over this into a grassy defile that runs between hedges beyond which, on the left, is an apple orchard, and, on the right, a colourful and well-tended garden.

You are heading in the direction of Nottingham Hill. You will pass a couple of gates to the left and right and you may have to negotiate a few nettles before arriving at a second stile at the end of the defile that faces a meadow that has appeared to the left.

Cross the stile into the meadow and turn immediately right. Head for a stile that you will see ahead of you around the corner and down across the field. Negotiate the stile, crossing a stream in the process, and enter a meadow which is effectively the slope of Nottingham Hill. Walk directly ahead in the direction of a stone wall you can see farther up the slope, which lies beyond the shrubs and bushes that are scattered roundabout. Behind you, you can see the bare buttocks of Cleeve Hill and a few houses dotted in its shadow. To your right are the remnants of another stone wall and beyond it more meadows and gateways.

Whilst you are to continue in the general direction of the summit of the slope, you do not go as far as the first-mentioned stone wall. Well before reaching it, you should make for the corner of a neighbouring field which will appear to the left. There you will see a wide gap between dense bramble which will take you into the field in question.

Turn immediately right, with hedge and tree to your right, and climb the slope towards trees and a gate. Behind you the views are opening up again, offering a clear view of the race course at Prestbury.

You will find that there is a sort of moveable railing to the right of the gate - use this to pass through but make sure that you return it so that it is flush against the hedgerow.

This takes you onto a wilder part of the hill, spiked in summer with a vast array of towering, purple-bobbed thistles. Ahead of you is what appears to be the summit of Nottingham Hill. The slope is covered with scrubby trees but there is only one tree of any substance and that is ahead of you on the crest of the hill. Head for this, threading your way gingerly through the thistles; and taking time to enjoy the view behind - the basin created by the meeting of two hills, and beyond, Cheltenham.

As you approach the tree, you will discover that it is stumpier and less vigorous than it seemed - an exaggerated bonsai tree. Near it is a log which, with its convenient indentation, makes a welcome resting place. Pass to the left of the tree and head in the general direction of the leftermost of two telegraph poles that are before you.

Beneath the poles is a stone wall. Away to your left is a gate set between wooden railings and bearing a yellow arrow - ignore this, and instead head for a corner of the stone wall beneath the aforementioned telegraph pole, next to a small shed which is just visible in a neighbouring field. Head for this corner to the right of the shed and there you will find a stone stile which you cross into a small field.

Cross this mossy field, towards a house with a brick chimney and you will quickly come to another stile and a metalled lane. Turn left and then, after a few yards, right, over a signposted break in a stone wall. This will drop you onto a grassy path that cuts a swathe up the slope slightly to the left - there is another going right, nearer the house, which you ignore - until you come to a gate.

Once through the gate walk up to a crossroads of grassy tracks and bear left around the crown of the hill. After about 15 yards turn right up a rising track and shortly, where it meets another track, bear left. Follow this through little mountains of bush and bramble towards some woodland you see ahead of you to the right. Well above you to the right you see a stone wall and a gate.

Soon, just as the track bears left and round and down towards the vale, cut off to the right and go over a gate into the woods. You will find yourself on a cool, clear path through thick woodland. The path widens and narrows, rises and falls but remains essentially straightforward, whilst around it there is a jungle of bramble, and spindly trees held in place by a plethora of creepers and roots.

One or two paths may tempt you down to the left; but ignore these and keep to the straight path until it brings you to a stile where the wood meets open hillside, and more magnificent views. Follow the path across the beam of the hill, with the ramparts of the Iron Age fort dating from approximately 600 BC - at 100 acres, one of the largest in the country - above you to the right. Beneath these mounds will be tall, dry stone walls, and, perhaps, the remains of round and rectangular buildings.

Ahead of you is a gate at the edge of an area of low trees. This will take you onto a track which descends slightly and will bring you soon enough to another gate. On the other side of the gate is another open area of hillside and beyond it more views to make your spirits soar, a shallow, flat canyon running between a series of escarpment buttresses. Below, to the left, are the remains of a farm, and two large cylindrical containers.

Go forward to a stony track and turn right. This rises to a gate. Go through onto a clear track that runs across the spine of the hill ahead of you. The fine views towards Winchcombe continue to the left; whilst to the right, if you are lucky enough to hit the right time of year, the fields will be bright with red poppies.

It will not be long before you catch glimpses of the radio masts of Cleeve Hill ahead of you. Then you will pass through an area of woodland - ignore all paths to the left and right - and a gateway until you reach another gate at the corner of a metalled lane. Keep straight on towards Cleeve, with familiar views to the right, and ahead of you on the course, golfers with their carts. You will come to the main road. On the other side is the road that leads up to the golf course clubhouse, open to the public for refreshment.

To return to your starting point turn right here onto the pavement and descend gently, passing the High Roost pub on the left and then an old milestone.

The Swallow

Collared Dove in flight

Rabbits running for cover into their burrow.

The Stoate

Meadow Buttercup

The NOTTINGHAM HILL Walk

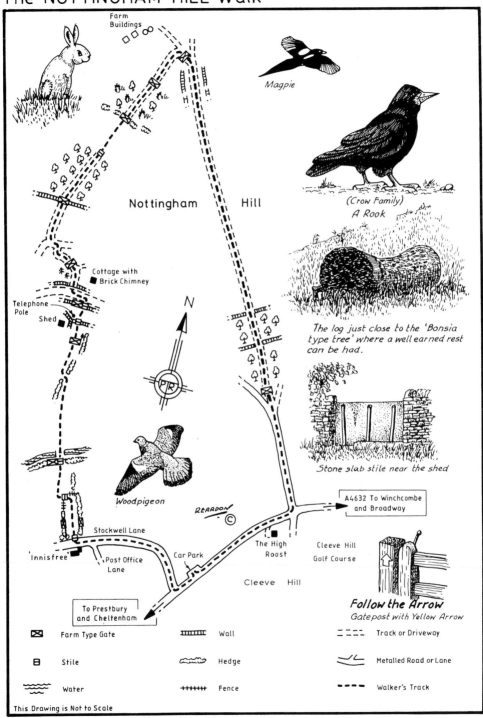

Farm Buildings

Magpie

(Crow Family)
A Rook

Nottingham Hill

Cottage with
Brick Chimney

Telephone
Pole

Shed

N

The log just close to the 'Bonsia type tree' where a well earned rest can be had.

Stone slab stile near the shed

Woodpigeon

REARDON ©

A4632 To Winchcombe
and Broadway

Stockwell Lane

Innisfree

Post Office
Lane

Car Park

The High
Roost

Cleeve Hill
Golf Course

Cleeve   Hill

Follow the Arrow
Gatepost with Yellow Arrow

To Prestbury
and Cheltenham

✉	Farm Type Gate	▥	Wall	‑‑‑‑	Track or Driveway
🅱	Stile	〰	Hedge	⌣⌐	Metalled Road or Lane
〰	Water	✛✛✛	Fence	‑ ‑ ‑	Walker's Track

This Drawing is Not to Scale

4. Adlestrop

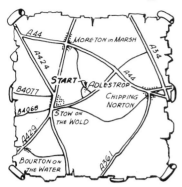

Distance: 3.5 miles

Time: 1hr 45mins continuous walking

Map: OS Pathfinder 1068 (SP22/32, Chipping Norton and Adlestrop).

Starting Point: Grid ref 242273

Terrain: Field and track with some woodland. Some mud. Only one short ascent.

Refreshments: No pub in Adlestrop, but the post office sells soft drinks. The Fox at Broadwell is nearby.

SOONER or later you are sure to land in Adlestrop, scene of one of the most striking of short modern poems. Regrettably, there is no pub or tea room in Adlestrop (although refreshment can be found within a short drive) but the walk is one of those that is so strangely satisfying that the omission is of little moment.

You are recommended to park in the village hall car park which is clearly signposted on the left as you enter the village coming from the direction of Stow. Leave the car park and turn left. You are confronted by a road junction and a bus shelter, with the name Adlestrop emblazoned across its back wall. This originally decorated the railway station, closed, sadly, since 1964. The preservation of the name plate, along with a station bench, is no mere piece of idle sentimentalising - for the fixture is almost a tangible part of English literature. The poet Edward Thomas passed through the village on a train during the First World War and the poem describes a moment which for many people sums up an English summer day and for many others speaks of much that is missed since the closure of branch railway lines. There is added poignancy for Thomas himself, who never set foot in the village, was to die in Flanders in 1917.

> 'Yes, I remember Adlestrop -
> The name because one afternoon,
> Of heat the express-train drew up there
> Unwontedly. It was late June.
>
> The steam hissed. Someone cleared his throat.
> No-one left and no-one came
> On the bare platform. What I saw
> Was Adlestrop - only the name.
>
> And willows, willow-herb, and grass,
> And meadowsweet and haycocks dry,
> No whit less still and lonely fair
> Than the high cloudlets in the sky.
>
> And for that minute a blackbird sang
> Close by, and around him, mistier,
> Farther and farther, all the birds
> Of Oxfordshire and Gloucestershire.

Having turned left out of the village hall, turn immediately left along a grassy track with hedgerow or trees at each side and which leads towards a modern farm building. The countryside here is flattish but surrounded on all sides by low, shallow slopes, like the bottom of a saucer. The lane passes the farm building on the left and enters into a large field, beyond which there are sloping fields and to the left of them, a copse. It is indeed quiet here with little sign of habitation – and the poem rings true, even in winter.

Keep to the right hand margin of the field, close to the blackberry (of good flavour) clad hedge. The track swings to the right and leads you to a stile. Once over the stile you have a choice of paths - one leads straight ahead across the field towards a farm. The other, the one you want, leads diagonally left across the bumps that are the legacy of medieval ridge and furrow ploughing techniques.

Sail across the bumps to the hedge and bear right, with the hedge to your left, and carry on to the corner where, perhaps partially hidden, is another stile by a hunting gate. Go through into another field. In front of you is an old barn and to the left another stile. Cross this to be at the base of a sloping furrowed, field with a gnarled, solitary tree at its centre and ruined buildings at the top to the right. Turn right to pass another tree, the barn on the right beyond a broken stone wall and then a hedge with leafy poll. You will eventually reach another gate and stile.

Pass through into another large field and head up the field in the direction of a gate you will be able to see at the edge of thin woodland dominated by a large tree. The ruined barn is visible still to the left; and after you have made a few steps the view behind you improves with surprising alacrity, as the gradation of shadow and colour varies all the way to the hills in the distance.

ADLESTROP HOUSE

REARDON

17

Crossing the stile will leave you on a path that continues to ascend through the trees until it levels out at the edge of a field. The path across should be more or less visible amid the crop but if it is not bear slightly right and head across until you cross a hedgeless boundary into another field, where you follow the same line over the brow of the hill - in fact the farmer here has kindly made the path more than obvious. The view to the left is grand, across the Vale of Evesham to the Malvern Hills.

The path fetches you up at an attractive wrought iron gate which leads you into a pasture. In front of you is Chastleton House, once owned by Robert Catesby, a conspirator in the Gunpowder Plot. Within its Jacobean walls is a secret room where a fugitive from the Battle of Worcester hid when Cromwell's men stormed the house. It boasts an attractive Long Gallery and topiary garden. The nearby church has some attractive medieval floor tiles.

Once in the pasture turn right to follow a path that hugs close to the edge of Peasewell Wood on the right. Across the field to the left is an unusually striking stone dovecot.

The path quickly brings you to a gate which leads into the wood. Pass through and follow the track as it bears right and left up through the trees, ignoring a gate at a corner. The path widens to a ride until at the top it bears right to debouch at the corner of a minor road. On your right is a stile. Go over that and follow a track as it bears around woodland to the left.

The track goes comfortably straight along the side of a hill with pasture sloping gently up to woodland on the left and falling away to trees and the vale on the right. Carry on as the roof of a barn appears ahead of you to the left and then, after some time, a bench and a small topograph rather surprisingly appear on the right.

The track soon bears slightly right past a tree and then approaches another tree at the corner of a square expanse of wood. To the right, half way down the slope is a telegraph pole. At the corner of the wood the track wheels around to the left, but you should carry straight on, keeping to the right of the wood. Pass this impenetrable wood, and a path with arrows which will appear on the left, until you come to a corner. Ignore the path straight ahead and instead turn sharp right down the field, with hedge on the left, to a gate that leads into more woodland.

Once in the wood, go ahead, ignoring other paths to the right and left, along a dead straight Roman road of a path. It may be rather muddy and you may find alternative paths running parallel to the main one. Eventually the main path narrows to a ribbon which will take you down to a gate at a road.

Go through and turn right. Walk on towards a corner and follow the road as it turns left and descends towards Adlestrop. As you proceed you will notice across to the right the ruined barn you saw near the beginning; and then you will come to a road on the left. Take this as it passes a number of attractive cottages. It comes to a corner - with a hedge in the shape of a gigantic snail - where the road bears right. Follow it down to a junction by a thatched house, which turns out to be a post office. By carrying on past this you will return to the bus stop and the village hall car park; but, if you wish, you may make a diversion by following the road on the left, just before the post office, which takes you to the church and 17th century Adlestrop House which was once occupied by an uncle of Jane Austen, Theophilus Leigh, who was rector here between 1718 and 1762. She was staying with him in Adlestrop when he heard that he had inherited Stoneleigh Hall, now the seat of the Royal Agricultural Society; and she accompanied him on his first visit there.

The ADLESTROP Walk

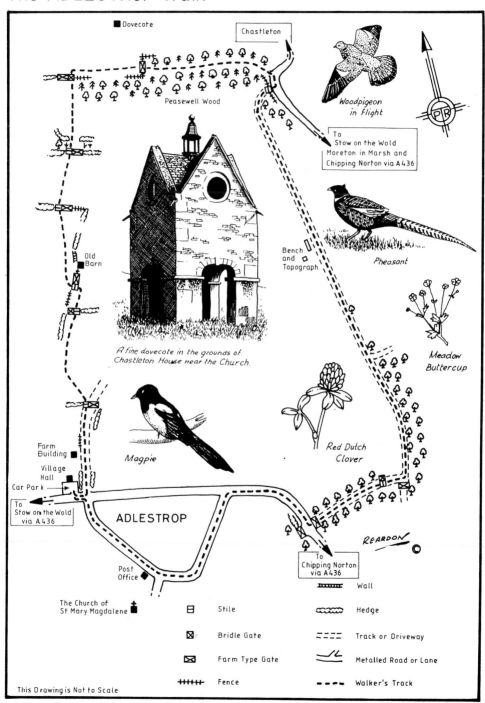

■ Dovecote

Chastleton

Peasewell Wood

Woodpigeon
in flight

To
Stow on the Wold
Moreton in Marsh and
Chipping Norton via A436

Pheasant

Old
Barn

Bench
and
Topograph

Meadow
Buttercup

A fine dovecote in the grounds of
Chastleton House near the Church.

Farm
Building

Village
Hall
Car Park

To
Stow on the Wold
via A436

Magpie

Red Dutch
Clover

ADLESTROP

REARDON

To
Chipping Norton
via A436

Post
Office

The Church of
St Mary Magdalene

☐	Stile	▦▦▦▦	Wall
⊠	Bridle Gate	◌◌◌◌	Hedge
⊠	Farm Type Gate	= = = =	Track or Driveway
++++++	Fence	⌣⌣	Metalled Road or Lane
		▬ ▬ ▬	Walker's Track

This Drawing is Not to Scale

5. Dowdeswell

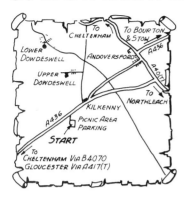

Distance: 3.75 miles

Time: 1hr 30mins continuous walking

Map: OS Pathfinder (1090 Northleach & Andoversford SP01/11) and 1089 Gloucester SO 81/91. Or Landranger series no.163 (Ch'm and Gloucester).

Starting Point: Grid ref 003186

Terrain: Field and track with a little road. Fairly flat with one brief descent.

Refreshments: Kilkenny Inn on the A436

THIS one is short and very sweet. It is ideal for a warm summer day, for the terrain is undemanding; but it offers much in a short space of time, particularly in the way of panoramic views. Dowdeswell lies a short way outside Cheltenham between the A40 and the A436.

Since parking space is at a premium in this area, the walk begins from the Kilkenny viewpoint car park which is located right on the A436, across the fields from Dowdeswell.

From the car park walk back down to the main road. Cross it and just a fraction to the right is a gate by a footpath sign. Go through the gate into a field. Keep very carefully to the left hand margin, in the shadow of a high, thick hedge, and follow it as it slopes gently downwards. Fine views towards Cheltenham develop to the left whilst, to the right, Dowdeswell Manor and a cluster of houses can be espied.

You will soon pass into another field. Once again keep to the left edge until you reach a small gate which will lead you to a grassy layby and a narrow country lane. Turn left here. The lane begins to descend a little, as it passes an open wedge-shaped meadow to the right. Straight ahead, more fields rise up before you towards patches of woodland. Not long after leaving the hedgeless meadow you will pass a patch of woodland and then a signposted footpath to the right, which is to be ignored. Then the track begins to gently ascend, passing another field on the right-hand side, perhaps with a track cutting across the corn. More views open up to the right across the valley to Dowdeswell Wood, and to Cheltenham and the hills beyond. Then, some little way before the buildings of Castle Barn Farm in front of you, you will come to a stone wall running away to the right at a right-angle, and a footpath sign. So turn right at the wall, and walk along a sort of track at the edge of a field, with the stone wall, and hedge, on your left. The track descends fairly gently, and leaving the field runs between two areas of dense hedgerow and shrub. This track, green and grassy, and therefore prone to mud on occasion, continues downwards. Ignore any turnings to the left and right and simply stroll on along this short and unspoilt rural cloister.

The track ends at a sort of junction of tracks with, ahead of you, a field. Go into the field and keep to its left hand margin, ignoring a gateway to the left. Continue to the apex of the field where you will come to an area of hedgerow and nettle to both left and right, a defile through which leads to a swing gate. Go through to where you will notice a cottage to your left. There are still more stupendous views of Lower Dowdeswell to the right and, to the left, of Dowdeswell Reservoir and far beyond. Just this side of the reservoir you may, if the foliage permits, be able to catch a glimpse of the half-timbered features of Rossley Gate house. However, this fifteenth century house did not start life here - it was originally in Cheltenham town, at the corner of Arle Avenue and Gloucester Road. But in 1929 it was bought for a few hundred pounds and then moved by a man who had inherited Rossley Manor and who wanted a stylish gatehouse for it. It stands close to the old embankment of the former Banbury to Cheltenham Direct Railway, opened in 1887 and closed in 1962. This was a passenger line but also transported coal from Wales, and iron ore to Wales. It also gave access for farmers to the important cattle market at Banbury.

The Kilkeney Inn, near Dowdeswell, Glos.

Go through another gate to the edge of a sloping field. Head down in the general direction of a pair of large trees at its centre. Pass to the right of them and then head towards the woodland beneath the church and houses of Lower Dowdeswell. Keep on a line a little to the left of the church as you look at it and roughly at the middle point of the woodland in order to discover at the base of the field a small metal gate among the trees that will lead to the edge of a secluded lawn.

Keep straight on taking care to keep to the very edge of the lawn - there may be an electric fence on your right to guide you - in the direction of a large house which you will see ahead of you outside the woods up the slope of a meadow. The path goes between some bushes, passes over a stream and fetches you up by a gate and a stile. Pass over into the meadow, with a pond on the left, and head up towards a gate to the right of the garden of the aforementioned house.

Pass through the gate into a sort of corral with a stone wall on the left and the sight of the church to the right. Cross a track and continue up to another gate with a walker's gate to its right. Pass through onto a gravel drive to the left of the old tithe barn and head up to the road.

Turn right along the grass bank and then follow a path through the churchyard, with the church itself to the left. The church (with dovecots in the four panels of its spire) is prettily

21

located in an attractive graveyard, where those who fell in the Great War are commemorated with rose bushes. Bear left around the church and then up some steps to the road.

Directly opposite is a footpath sign; but ignore this and instead turn right along the road for a good two hundred yards until you come to another footpath sign attached to a post opposite some cottages, pointing across the road.

Turn left to cross the road and follow the track that runs beside the cottages to their right. Very shortly there is an entrance to a field on the left - ignore that and continue ahead to its right, passing to the left of a cottage and through its grounds. You will enter a cool defile between bushes and trees which will take you past the rusting carcass of a car. The path takes you to a gate at the edge of a field.

Keep straight on along the right hand margin of this field, to the left of a grassy mound, without entering the neighbouring field to the right. In the distance ahead of you to the left is visible the mansion of Sandywell Park, once described by Horace Walpole, a little unfairly, as 'a square box of a house, very dirtily situated'. As you approach the end of the field you will notice a high stone wall peeping over the hedge. Just before it is a stile. Go over this on to the metalled lane where you turn right. Proceed along here as it rises a little, passing Andoversford and Dowdeswell Burial Ground to the left in the process. Eventually you will come to a larger road at a junction - cross this onto another minor road to continue by a barn joined to a house on the right.

After some three hundred yards you will come to a turning on the right which leads to the village of Upper Dowdeswell. At this point you have a choice. If you desire refreshment, then continue forward along the road, passing the entrance to the village, until after about three hundred and fifty yards, you come to the Kilkenny pub. Then you can return to the village.

Take the road into Upper Dowdeswell, passing a few houses of fairly recent construction, before entering the heart of the old village with a series of venerable, low cottages on the right (one of which was the old schoolhouse). The name of the village apparently comes from a Saxon chief by the name of Dodo who, along with another chief called Odo, founded Tewkesbury.

Pass a track leading down to the right, and an old well on the left, with the sculpted figure of an animal - a deer perhaps - within and an inscription referring to the donation of the well by a benefactor in 1870. Ignore another track leading away to the right, pass more cottages on the left and proceed to where the road opens up in front of the fetching Upper Dowdeswell Manor (once noted as 'one of the most delightful of Cotswold houses'), which dates back to the late sixteenth century and is now divided into flats.

Pass the manor on your left and follow the road as it passes some cottages, and then, on the right, a small gate, and magnificent views to Cheltenham across the meadows below which, to judge from the arrangement of the trees, were originally estate parkland.

The road becomes more of a lane now, with grass running along its back and hedgerows along each side. Across the meadows to the left of you the Kilkenny mast is visible, and the lane is soon accompanied by a stone wall on the right.

Shortly, on the left, you will notice the grass lay-by and the gate into a field that you came through earlier. Pass through again and retrace your steps back up the fields to the main road and the car park.

The KILKENNY - DOWDESWELL Walk

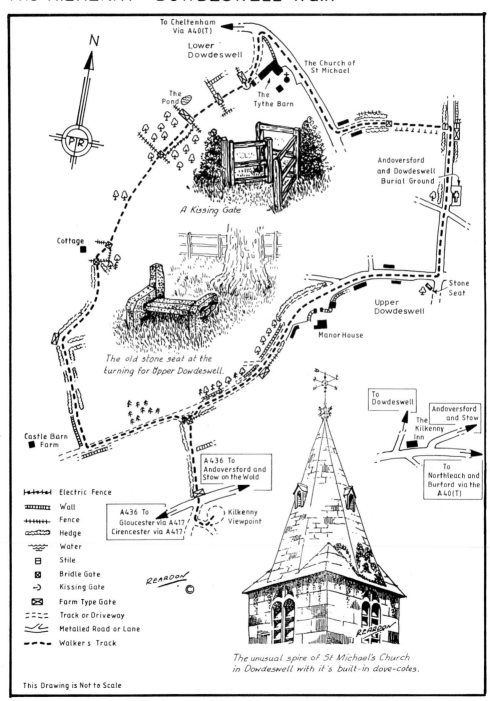

N

PR

To Cheltenham Via A40(T)

Lower Dowdeswell

The Church of St Michael

The Pond

The Tythe Barn

A Kissing Gate

Andoversford and Dowdeswell Burial Ground

Cottage

The old stone seat at the turning for Upper Dowdeswell.

Stone Seat

Upper Dowdeswell

Manor House

Castle Barn Farm

To Dowdeswell

The Kilkenny Inn

Andoversford and Stow

A436 To Andoversford and Stow on the Wold

To Northleach and Burford via the A40(T)

A436 To Gloucester via A417 Cirencester via A417

Kilkenny Viewpoint

REARDON ©

╂╂╂	Electric Fence
▥▥▥	Wall
++++++	Fence
∽∽∽	Hedge
∿∿	Water
∏	Stile
▨	Bridle Gate
⌐)	Kissing Gate
⊠	Farm Type Gate
⁼⁼⁼⁼	Track or Driveway
⌁	Metalled Road or Lane
▬ ▬ ▬	Walker s Track

REARDON

The unusual spire of St Michael's Church in Dowdeswell with it's built-in dove-cotes.

This Drawing is Not to Scale

23

6. Northleach/Hampnett

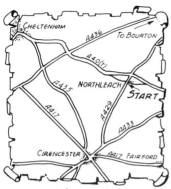

Distance: 4 miles

Time: Nearly 2hrs of continuous walking

Map: OS Pathfinder SP 01/11 Northleach and Andoversford

Starting Point: Grid ref 112146

Terrain: Muddy fields and tracks and a little road. Mostly flat with a few mild gradients.

Refreshments: Plenty of pubs and tea shops in Northleach.

THIS walk would be ideal for a freezing day when the furrows are frosted hard and the puddles glazed with ice. It may also be of interest to anyone who has ever seen the sign to Hampnett on the Oxford road and wondered about it. The walk begins and ends in Northleach, one of the most interesting towns in the Cotswolds, which lies half way between Cheltenham and Burford on the A40.

Close to Northleach church is the Market Place, where there is ample space for parking . This is an attractive square, surrounded by shops, inns, a post office and, close by, public lavatories. Northleach, bypassed by the A40 now and so returned to the comparative peace of former times, is untypical of the Cotswolds, with its variety of architectural styles, much of it seemingly Regency inspired, yet built in local stone.

The town is dominated by its church, an excellent example of the Perpendicular style and one of the three finest wool churches in the Cotswolds (the others being at Cirencester and Chipping Campden). It is worth a visit, perhaps before commencing the walk.

Northleach came into existence in 1220 when grants for a weekly market and annual fairs were granted by Henry III. The main business was in wool, mostly with Italy at first and then with Bruges; and although there had been a church in Northleach from at least the early 13th century, the current one dates largely from the 15th century, thanks to the generosity of wealthy local woolmen. Their participation in a concerted effort means that much of the church dates from the same period and is in a homogeneous style (apart from the tower, which dates from the 14th century). Indeed, the church smacks of ambition, as if it were the chapel of a small university. Within is one of the finest collections of brasses in the country, mostly in memory of the merchants who built the church.

To begin the walk, turn left from the Market Place, with your back to the post office, and walk past the War Memorial in the direction of the A429. In so doing you will pass a variety of architectural styles, including a half-timbered house, unusual for the Cotswolds. Many of the houses, and the streets or alleys, have evocative and unusual names: Doctor's Lane, Malt Cottage and so on. Pass the Cotswold Hall on the left, with its clock, a cottage with an old bell pull, and then cross to the other side of the road, pass a workshop where the art of stained glass manufacture flourishes and follow a path which runs between two rows of trees.

The path debouches at the main road by a petrol station. Opposite you, on the other side of the road is a fortress of a building, which houses the Cotswold Countryside Collection, a museum devoted to the history of agriculture in the Cotswold area, built mainly around the Lloyd-Baker collection of implements and wagons. The building itself has an interesting history, for this was once a police station and prison built in 1790 by the eccentrically named Sir Onesiphorus Paul, who maintained an interest in penal reform and prisoner welfare. This prison, with exercise yard and separate rooms for sleeping, bathing and medical attention, was revolutionary for its time. There was once a workhouse at the other side of Northleach which led to the gibe that one entered the town by the workhouse and left by the prison.

"THE RED LION" IN NORTHLEACH.

You too should leave Northleach by the prison, keeping it to your right by taking briefly the road between it and the restaurant opposite. Almost immediately you will come to a stile on the right. Take this, which will permit you a glimpse into the yard of the museum, and drop towards the prison wall. Here beginneth the mud. Follow the wall by bearing left and then right until you come to the infant River Leach. Turn left and follow the margin of the field, with the river on the right, until you come to a small, flat bridge at the corner. Turn right to cross it and immediately left. In the distance is a large house and to the right, across the field, are the trees, with tops of crew-cut evenness, of Prison Copse.

Follow the margin of the field in the direction of a gate you will see ahead; on your left will be tumble-down stone walls and beyond them the Leach. As you continue forward, the church and houses of Hampnett will appear ahead of you.

Pass through the gate and then head towards another gate and beside it a stile. If the ground is wet you may find that the higher ground provides easier walking. Behind you Northleach church remains visible, as indeed it does for almost all of the walk. Cross the stile into another field. The next stile is invisible over the brow of the hill but by keeping just to the right of the big house as you cross the field, you will come to it. Or you can turn immediately right as you enter the field and follow the margin of the field.

The stile takes you onto a track. If you wish to visit Hampnett and its church, turn right and follow the track up to the road, after which you should return to this point. Hampnett is the site of the source of the Leach and of a pretty church with an interesting interior that is

25

not to everyone's taste; to quote an earlier guidebook 'a lovely and structurally little-spoiled Norman building, it is, however, a most damning indictment of uninspired enthusiasm, for its walls and ceilings have been so covered with stencilling as to recall the efforts of an eccentric tattoo artist'. This work, an attempt to recreate similar work popular in the Middle Ages, was accomplished in the 1880s. There are some finely carved birds on the capitals supporting chancel arch. The vicars of the 18th Century here were well-known for marrying couples without asking too many questions.

Return down the track and pass the stile you crossed on the left. The track curves right, crosses the Leach which pours down from the right, passes beneath the big house, crosses a muddy farmyard and comes to a junction where you turn left. The track climbs steadily out of an amphitheatre of green towards a gate; go through, using the metal loop pull kindly provided, and continue to climb until you meet another gate. Go through this and cross the road in front of you onto a track at the margin of a field to the left of a stone wall.

By now you are on a plateau with views extending quite some distance, particularly on your left. Ahead of you is a giant pylon, part of a long line that closes ranks farther on to the left and marches inexorably across the fields. Keep to the main grassy track and pass through another gateway. Soon you will pass some utility works on the left and emerge onto a minor metalled road.

Turn left here and walk on. You will pass a crossroads - to Northleach and Stow-on-the-Wold to the left and Yanworth to the right - but continue on until you come to the main road. You must cross this, and take great care in the process, because the traffic moves quickly. This is the A429 again, once the Roman Fosse Way, the best known of the Roman roads in Britain. Built in 60AD, it ran between Exeter and Lincoln and marked the first Roman invasion and consolidation of advances made in the south of England. Some time later a Saltway was established just to the south to transport salt from Droitwich to London via Lechlade.

Go through a bridle gate on the far side of the road to find yourself on a grass track at the edge of a field. Follow this track, with a stone wall on the left, towards farm buildings you see in the distance ahead of you. It curves a little to the left and then becomes a track fenced in by hedgerow and trees. You kink left and right into the farmyard and head straight ahead towards a track with a grass spine, passing cottages on the right and attractive farm buildings on the left.

As this track approaches its end you will catch sight of the crenellations of Northleach church tower to the left. Then you will come to another road. Cross this and enter the leftermost of the tracks before you. Follow this along its muddy way for about a quarter of a mile until you come to a large break in the hedge on the left, where the stone wall comes out to an end, and just after a point where a couple of trees, separated by about 100 yards, have become detached from their fellows on the right, having ventured towards the middle of the track.

Turn left through the gap into a field alongside a stone wall. Below you is Northleach, glowing in the setting sun if you should be walking in the late afternoon. Continue down to a stile. Cross this into a meadow and head slightly to the right of the church. You will come to a sort of ladder stile and then a steep bank - if you find this a little daunting, turn right here and follow the margin of the field towards a play area, where there is a small gate. Go through, pass the tennis courts and head for the white gate at the other end of the playing field. Head for the road, turn right and make your way back to the town centre.

The NORTHLEACH - HAMPNETT Walk

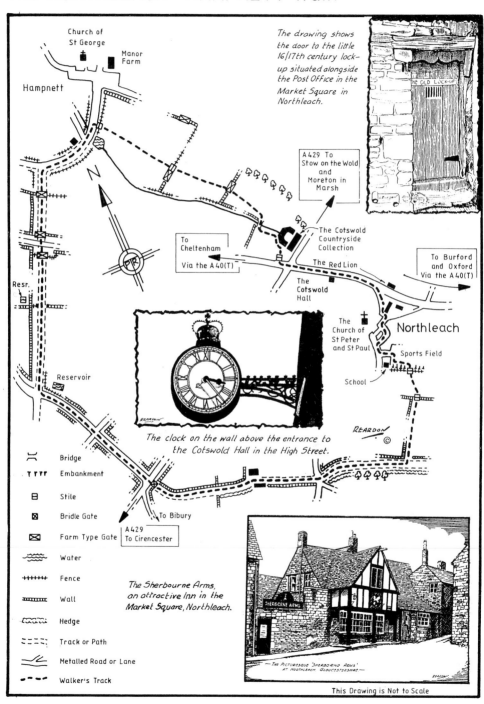

Church of St George

Manor Farm

Hampnett

The drawing shows the door to the little 16/17th century lock-up situated alongside the Post Office in the Market Square in Northleach.

THE OLD LOCK-UP

A429 To Stow on the Wold and Moreton in Marsh

To Cheltenham Via the A40(T)

The Cotswold Countryside Collection

The Red Lion

The Cotswold Hall

The Church of St Peter and St Paul

To Burford and Oxford Via the A40(T)

Northleach

Sports Field

School

Reservoir

REARDON ©

The clock on the wall above the entrance to the Cotswold Hall in the High Street.

Resr.

⌣ Bridge

ⲧⲧⲧⲧ Embankment

🅱 Stile

⊠ Bridle Gate

⊠ Farm Type Gate

〜〜 Water

+++++ Fence

▭▭▭ Wall

〰〰 Hedge

〓〓 Track or Path

〜〜 Metalled Road or Lane

▬ ▬ ▬ Walker's Track

To Bibury

A429 To Cirencester

The Sherbourne Arms, an attractive Inn in the Market Square, Northleach.

— THE PICTURESQUE 'SHERBORNE ARMS' AT NORTHLEACH GLOUCESTERSHIRE —

SHERBORNE ARMS

This Drawing is Not to Scale

27

7. Southrop/Eastleach

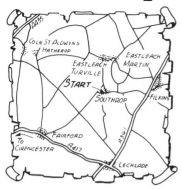

Distance: 4.25 miles

Time: 2hrs 30mins continuous walking

Map: OS Pathfinder 1115 (SP20/30 Witney, Carterton), OS P'finder 1114 (C'cester SP00/10)

Starting Point: Grid ref 199035

Terrain: Track, road, field and riverside.No sharp gradients.

Refreshments: The Swan at Southrop and The Victoria at Eastleach.

THIS walk takes you to one of the most glowing corners of the Cotswolds, one which is at its best, it seems to me, on a crisp winter's day. In fact, try to select one of those days when the sky is frosted blue and time the walk for the late afternoon so that the sun is beginning to set as you reach the end when the shadows are long and the colours at their warmest. The walk includes a visit to the delightful twin villages of Eastleach Turville and Eastleach Martin. Southrop is 3.5 miles north east of Fairford.

In the pretty village of Southrop, park in the vicinity of the Swan, which is concealed beneath a dense mat of creeper. There is a bench outside and a little green at its side. Southrop has a fine 16th century manor house, and a tiny, Norman church, with a magnificent font, where John Keble, leader of the 19th century Oxford Movement was rector. Here he wrote much of his volume of verse 'The Christian Year' which was to become an Anglican 'High Church' vade mecum.

With the pub on your right, walk along the road in the direction of Fairford. The road curves left and right, passes a proper telephone box on the left and an attractive house where a character from a Jane Austen novel might have lived. On the right is the village hall. Pass a gateway on the left around the bend from two stone walls, new houses under construction on the right, and then ignore the road to Lechlade to the left as the Fairford road continues out of the village.

Pass the old well set into the wall, marked 1897, on the right hand side; and leave the nestling village as the road ascends slightly to a bend, where it turns sharp right and straightens up towards a distant farm building. A stile and playing field will appear on the right, followed by a culvert as companion to the road. Soon you will pass the farm building espied earlier on the left, followed by a cottage with a proper telephone box in its yard. Ahead of you the road curves left by a house and a signpost indicating Fairford to the left and Burford and Eastleach to the right. The fields undulate across the plateau before you to the right towards an enclosed area of woodland.

Straight across the road is a lane which runs to the right of the house. It descends through overspreading branches, vestiges of russet leaves clinging to them, its muddiness mitigated by its stoniness. The path levels out into the open and then rises again through more foliage. Shortly after, the main path appears to veer away to the left around some woodland; when in fact you are to keep straight ahead beneath the arching branches. The track rises up and narrows to a charming path flanked by bushes and brambles heavy with berries.

An open field will appear above you to the left beyond the bushes. After a while you will notice to the right, across the fields, a circular structure, like a tin humming top. Quite suddenly the path will bring you out into the open at a corner of a wide concrete strip. To the left is a pretty view to a church spire and a ratchet-shaped hill.

So bear right along what was a runway of a Second World War airfield, one of many that lay hidden in the Cotswolds. The runway passes plantation on the left, with some handsome Christmas trees, and then fields. The tin drum seen earlier will appear to the right, and perhaps a long row of round bales parcelled in black, ready to bust dams.

Eventually the runway comes to an end at a wide gateway by some trees, and a metalled lane. Turn right here and follow the road as it descends, after a while, between thick hedgerow to Hammersmith Bottom. Just where the field bottoms out, before a stream, turn right into a field. Once in the field, bear left and follow the left hand margin above the stream bed, around the thick trunk of a tree. To your right is what seems to be a large trough, next to a patch of improbable green. Further up to the right a solitary tree sprouts out of a green base.

After following the curve of the field for a short distance turn left through a gateway into another field. Follow its stony, left-hand margin as it rises alongside a hedge. At the top of the field you will come to a corner where, alarmingly, there seems no way through to the field beyond. In fact, among the branches, is a narrow bridge which will take you across to a short, overgrown path and bring you to the corner of the neighbouring field. Keep straight on in the direction of the enclosed woodland, seen earlier, at the top of the rise. As you approach the woodland there are broad views to the right, while roofs appear a couple of fields away.

Once you get to the woodland, keep to its left where runs a wide swathe of green. Ignore all entrances through the beautiful stone wall to the woods on the right and head for the buildings you see before you. As you leave the woods, you will pass an old windmill on the right. Follow the track to the left of the farm buildings and continue on, passing more buildings where slate roofing is produced, until you come to a road, where you turn left.

As you descend the road, passing a tree with brittle branches reaching up like coral, the roofs of Eastleach Turville will appear, in delightful array, below you. As you enter the village itself, with the clocktower at a corner on the right, the Victoria Inn, with its postage-stamp like sign, will arise on the raised bank on the far side of the road.

Turn right here and follow the road through the lovely village, until it curves left by the war memorial and descends towards the river. On your right you will pass a partially concealed power station, after which is the old clapper bridge (or Keble Bridge, for Keble was rector of both churches here as well) across the River Leach. Cross the bridge, although if you wish to have a look at Eastleach Turville church, you should stay this side and follow the road to the corner where you will see the church on the left. Then you can return to the clapper bridge, cross it and follow the path on the far side which will lead you to the gate of Eastleach Martin Churchyard. Go through the churchyard, with the church to the left and an old barn to the right until you come to another gate by a road.

Turn right here and follow the road as it heads on between two stone walls. At a bend

The Victoria Inn, in
Eastleach Turville

there is a track leading away to the left but keep to the road as it passes water meadows to the right, with views behind you to the Eastleaches. The river is never very far away and indeed it comes almost alongside the road at one point. Then you will come to some cottages on the right where the river appears to become subterranean, for it just disappears, briefly, only to reappear a little way beyond.

The road rises up gently. About a hundred yards after the cottage you will see a little bridge below you to the right, which you ignore. The road levels, descends, and you will catch sight of a cottage ahead of you. Keep going to where the road bends leftwards. You are looking for a path through the trees on the right - you will see it just where the road bends, before a telegraph pole. Some way beyond the pole, on the left, is a footpath sign.

So take the path on the right; it will lead you over or around a stile, and join the river on the right. Skip over a tree conveniently provided with steps and press on along a patch of green turf, with woodland away to the left. The houses of Fyfield will soon appear to the left. Follow the course of the river, cross a little wooden bridge stile over a rivulet, and continue until you reach another charming stone bridge ahead of you on the right. Just by it is a stile - cross it and turn right over the bridge, pausing only to play Poohsticks, for which it was obviously made.

Once over the bridge you will find yourself in a meadow rising up to the houses of Southrop. Walk up the slope and then cut diagonally leftwards to reach the top left-hand corner. Here are some iron bars - cross these, walk along the defile which passes between a delightful house to the right and an impressive dovecot to the left, until you reach a road. Turn left here and follow the road back to the Swan pub.

The SOUTHROP-EASTLEACH Walk

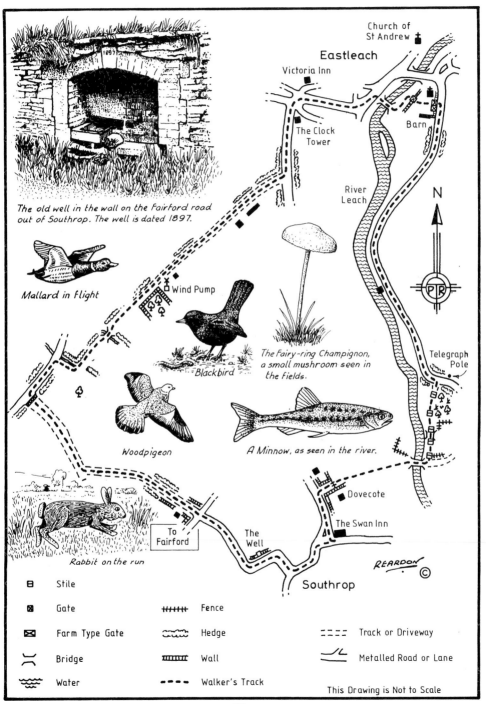

The old well in the wall on the Fairford road out of Southrop. The well is dated 1897.

Mallard in Flight

Wind Pump

Blackbird

Woodpigeon

The Fairy-ring Champignon, a small mushroom seen in the fields.

A Minnow, as seen in the river.

Rabbit on the run

Church of St Andrew

Eastleach

Victoria Inn

The Clock Tower

Barn

River Leach

N

Telegraph Pole

Dovecote

The Swan Inn

To Fairford

The Well

Southrop

REARDON ©

	Stile				
	Gate	┼┼┼┼┼	Fence		
	Farm Type Gate	〜〜〜	Hedge	＝＝＝＝	Track or Driveway
	Bridge	▥▥▥	Wall		Metalled Road or Lane
	Water	- - - -	Walker's Track		This Drawing is Not to Scale

31

8. Miserden/Winstone

Distance: 4.5 miles

Time: 2hr 15mins continuous walking

Map: OS Pathfinder 1113 (SO 80/90, Stroud)

Starting Point: Grid ref 936089

Terrain: Some sharp ascents and descents. Woodland paths, field margins, and a little road. Some mud.

Refreshments: The Carpenter's Arms at Miserden.

THIS walk is in one of those parts of the Cotswolds that always comes as a bit of a surprise - an area of considerable seclusion tucked away between two busy main roads. Miserden lies between the A46 and the A417, about four miles to the east of Painswick.

There are two places where you should have no problem in finding parking spaces - either close to the school, on the outskirts of the village, or opposite the church. The church, beyond its considerable yew arch like a bulky green magnet, standing in a particularly attractive churchyard, has Saxon origins. Inside there are a few things to be noted - some fine gilded, carved reredos and the exceptionally fine seventeenth century monument in the south choir to Sir William Sandys and his wife Margaret.

With the church on your left, and the war memorial to your right, proceed towards the middle of this mostly nineteenth and early twentieth century estate village. The name of the village derives from Musard, the name of the family that held it in the twelfth and thirteenth centuries. As you go you will pass a number of neat cottages with colourful gardens, and views down the Frome Valley which open up to the left, before arriving at the village centre dominated by a spreading sycamore encircled with benches. Here too is a proper red telephone box and the Carpenter's Arms pub.

Bear left here down the hill towards a white gate that will appear directly in front of you. Go through this by means of the pedestrian entrance at its side and descend the metalled drive as it heads between stone walls towards the dense woodland below. There may well be horses grazing in this rolling meadow which is sparsely planted with trees. After about 150 yards, at a point where the drive meets a pair of trees, and curls left, strike off diagonally right over the brow of the hillside and down towards a stone stile inserted into a small opening in the woods. Below you to the left the drive flattens out and disappears.

Cross the stile onto a clear, narrow path through dense woodland bedecked with flowers, some of which seem to give out the warm aroma of garlic. The path rises slightly at first, before levelling out and eventually broadening to a perhaps muddy track which will descend to a metalled road. Do not go right, or behind you to the left, but take the farthest road ahead of you by turning left and quickly right.

The road is level and bears left around woodland. Pass a turning on the left, cross a bridge - over a clear brook and a moist water meadow, left - and keep to the road as it climbs Winstone Hill, ignoring all turnings into the woods, until, after some 250 yards, the road climbs sharply right. Here turn left into the woods along a rising grassy path for about forty yards, passing a stagnant pool on the right, and then turn sharp right.

The path takes you up to a broader track, which you cross to take the path which rises clearly, if sharply, up amid the trees until it comes to an end at a wall and stone stile, with ahead of you a field and to your left, over another wall at the edge of the wood, a meadow.

Cross the stile and turn sharply left at the edge of the field, with the meadow on your left, filled, perhaps, with sheep greeting you with baleful stares, and continue to the bridle gate at the road. Pass through and turn right. Walk along the road as it curves slightly and then look for a footpath sign for Winstone hidden on the left among some trees.

This will take you to the edge of a field. Follow it as it bears right towards some trees and then turn left and right - it is likely to be waymarked - into woods. Follow the obvious path along the edge of the wood, with the field just beyond it to the right, the air filled with the pungent smell of earth and greenery. You will emerge out of the trees at the corner of the field, with more woodland in front of you, and a track running away to the left. Bear right, between the woodland and the field, and then left, at which point you reenter the woods at the corner and continue along a path running parallel with the edge of the field. Watch out for the hidden perils of rabbit holes. Once again you will emerge at a corner where you should bear right into the field and then immediately left.

Across the fields to your right you see a small cottage and a farm. On your left a hedge grows out of the base of an old stone wall, periodically visible. Follow the edge of the field until you come to the corner. Enter the next field and turn immediately right, walking along its edge in the direction of Pound Cottage. To your left are open fields riding up to a brow crowned with a bushy spinney. By the cottage you will arrive at a gate - cross this and turn right past the cottage down to the road. To your left is the village of Winstone, its church complete with saddleback tower and part of a fourteenth century cross, should you care to visit.

POUND COTTAGE
AT WINSTONE

The Carpenters Arms ~ Miserden

The walk, however, continues by taking the road before you and then the first right, which will soon bring you directly to the gates of Miserden Park.

Pass through them and walk along the narrow asphalt road, flanked by broad verges and thin woodland, until it begins to dip down, revealing some of the buildings of Miserden Park beyond. Where the road bears sharply right towards two gateposts surmounted by a pair of proud eagles, you will be confronted by a bridle path that heads straight down towards the House. Take this, ignoring other paths that lead away to the left, as it descends fairly steeply, and continue on as it curls down, passing other tracks to the left and right, and at one point looping around a tree before levelling out beside the still, diesel coloured lake on the right, surrounded by woodland and sprinkled with coot. Soon you will pass a little bridge, right, arching over rushing water, and hear the steady beat of the pump. Immediately after you will come to a metalled tracked, before a wooden gate and a steep valley side, where you turn left, up a hill. Just as it levels out at the corner of the meadow, another track continues up to the right. Take this as it ascends into trees, passes a track to the left, and arrives at a gate. Pass into a meadow and continue straight on across it, sparing a glance for Miserden's Elizabethan mansion to the right. Carry on across, with behind you views of the lake lately passed and the surrounding forest of Siberian density, until you come to another gate. Go through to a road and turn left as it descends beneath a canopy of branches, subsides below a stone wall, and levels out into sunlight. The road bears left and right and just as it begins to rise again, you will see a footpath on the right, leading through a gate into a rising field.

Go through onto a track that leads up the saddle-shaped hill towards some trees. As the track fades away, continue along the same line towards the left corner of the trees and pass through a gate onto a path that continues to rise slightly until you meet a wide track where you turn right. The track still ascends gently, leaves the trees behind and enters more open country until you come to a sort of crossroads of fields, probably vividly waymarked. Turn sharp right here and follow the margin of the field, with a stone wall to the left. At the top left corner pass through a narrow cleft into another field and keep straight ahead until you come to a road. Cross this onto another path by means of a stone stile, with a stone wall this time on the right, and follow this until it crosses another stile, enters a defile between the pretty cottages of Miserden and fetches you up on the road below the sycamore tree. Turn left and wend your way back to the starting point.

The MISERDEN - WINSTONE Walk

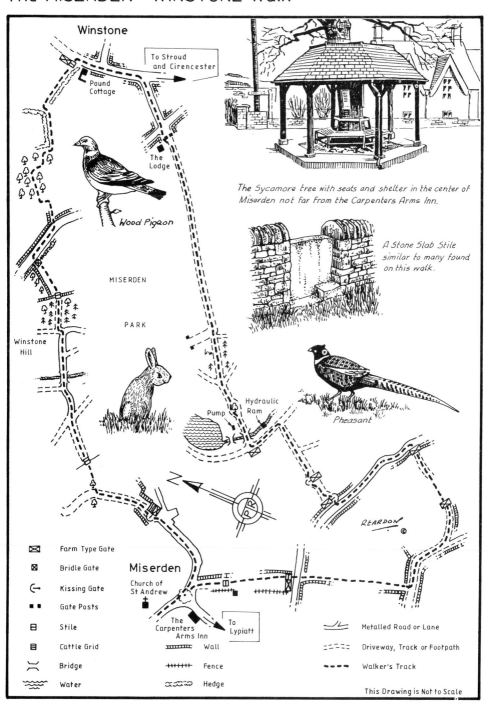

Winstone

To Stroud and Cirencester

Pound Cottage

The Lodge

Wood Pigeon

MISERDEN

PARK

Winstone Hill

Hydraulic Ram

Pump

Pheasant

REARDON ©

The Sycamore tree with seats and shelter in the center of Miserden not far from the Carpenters Arms Inn.

A Stone Slab Stile similar to many found on this walk.

Miserden

Church of St Andrew

The Carpenters Arms Inn

To Lypiatt

⊠	Farm Type Gate
⊗	Bridle Gate
↵	Kissing Gate
••	Gate Posts
⊟	Stile
⊟	Cattle Grid
⏝	Bridge
〰	Water

| Wall |
| Fence |
| Hedge |

| Metalled Road or Lane |
| Driveway, Track or Footpath |
| Walker's Track |

This Drawing is Not to Scale

9. Coln Rogers

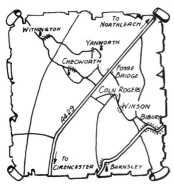

Distance: 5 miles

Time: 2hrs continuous walking

Map: OS Pathfinder SP 1/11 (Northleach & Andoversford) and OS Pathfinder SP 00/10 (Cirencester)

Starting Point: Grid ref 087094

Terrain: Generally flat with a few mild gradients.

Refreshments: Nearest pub is the Hare and Hounds, at Fosse Cross on the A429.

A walk of contrasting flavours. Two charming villages, slumbering on the banks of the Coln, are on the route, one of which boasts a delightful and much-ignored Saxon church. Another part takes you through a long and winding valley amid tremendous solitude, whilst a third takes you across beautiful exposed upland. Coln Rogers lies just to the east of the A429, some 6 miles north east of Cirencester.

Coln Rogers, though small, is spread over quite a large area. Parking should not prove much of a problem, but please be sure to park well off the road, on a verge for example, in such a way that nobody's path is obstructed. The village was originally Coln-on-the-Hills but the current name derives from the Norman knight, Roger de Gloucester who, anxious to save his soul as he lay wounded at Walyeson, granted the manor here to the monks of Gloucester. They renamed the village accordingly. The church here is of considerable interest and worth a visit; but since the route takes you past it as the walk comes to a close, more detailed mention is made at the end of this narrative.

The road passes through the village and bears left by means of a bridge over the Coln. The walk begins here. Cross the bridge and keeping to this quiet road, head for Winson. To your right the Coln races across a meadow, on the left it meanders towards a large country house - a sleepy pastoral scene.

You will enter Winson, which you see ahead of you, almost as soon as you have left Coln Rogers. Having past the village hall of Coln Rogers on the left, and after noticing that you are walking along the bottom of a shallow valley the sides of which are made up of choppy little fields, you will pass the signpost marking the entrance to Winson. On your right is a meadow, grazed perhaps by long-haired sheep with nicely-shaped horn, and beyond, signs of the old mill.

The road veers sharply to the right by the rampant guardians of Winson Mill Farm, crosses the river yet again by, on the left, a pretty ornamental garden, and, opposite, the old mill. Then the road bears left again and cuts upwards between steep banks towards more houses. As it reaches them, it flattens out and looks down to the valley and farm buildings on the left and passes a number of attractive gardens in the process. Just after two large modernised buildings on the left, the road curves away to the right at a point where you should bear left towards the village centre and the church.

The centre of the village is a triangular green, overlooked by a large and stately home.

The church, with its highly decorated chancel, is nearby. Winson, by the way, is noted for having the smallest post office in the West Country (so small I could not find it). Bear left past some cottages, then pass a barn and proper red telephone box, and follow the road as it narrows between two stone walls and runs in front of a series of highly attractive cottages, among them one that is thatched.

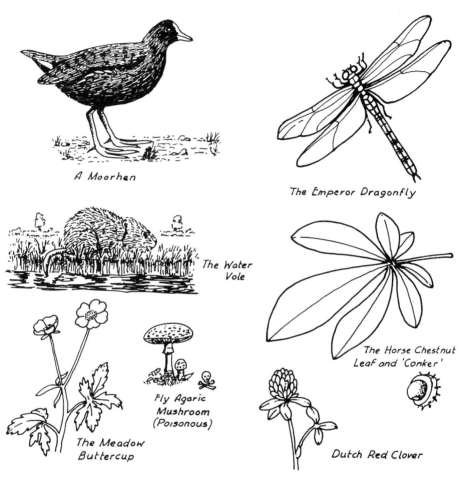

A Moorhen

The Emperor Dragonfly

The Water Vole

The Horse Chestnut Leaf and 'Conker'

Fly Agaric Mushroom (Poisonous)

The Meadow Buttercup

Dutch Red Clover

Well before that, however, you will pass a cottage covered in creepers, with another pair of fearsome guardians at its wrought iron gates. Immediately after, on the left, is a concrete marker and a white gate. Pass through this and head for another white gate you see before you, which leads over a pair of stone slabs and then to a wooden footbridge across the river.

Follow the obvious, peaty, path through a grove of trees towards a plantation of fir. The path leads through the firs towards a gate at the edge of a field, before which the path bears right between the trees and the field and leads up to a stile and a stone wall. On the other side of the stile you will find yourself at the edge of another field. Bear left up and across the field through a scattering of bushes and trees to the far corner. As you go up the village of Winson will become visible behind you across the tops of the trees.

In the corner there is a gateway, difficult to miss because of a large yellow arrow painted onto a tree. Below you a farm track falls away to a steep sided valley. Follow the track down and then turn left along the valley bottom. On your right the side of the valley is steep and ribbed, on the left it slopes more gently. The path threads its way along the bed. It is like a river without water; and at every corner, you almost expect a deluge to rush at you. Certainly, there is a consuming feeling of solitude here and the chances are that the only sound you will hear in almost total silence is that of birdsong.

So charge on until you come to a wall and pass through a gate, steering around the base of a steep outcrop that falls away from Dead Man's Acre Copse. Continue walking along the valley bottom until, eventually, as the valley tapers to a head, you will see a barn ahead of you. Ignore the entrance to a field on the left, with its steeplechase jumps, and pass a row of trees on the right in the direction of the barn. The track takes you through a gate, passes the enclosure and barn on the left and then passes through yet another gate. Ahead to the right another copse rises from behind a stone wall.

The track will begin to rise slightly as it heads towards more woodland lying beyond a hill shaped like an upturned boat. You will pass this woodland on the left; just as it ends the track bears sharply right. Ignore this and instead continue directly ahead, briefly, until it turns left through a gate into a field. With a stone wall on your right, follow the track until you come to a road. The view up here is substantially different, for you have reached a plateau and the view is extensive, with a skyline shaped by the silhouette of distant trees.

Once you reach the road, turn left. Take care here, even if there is but little traffic. As the road descends, you will see on the left the valley you recently left, and its interlocking shoulders. Then the road descends still further, passes an attractive house on the right, set back from the road, followed by a cottage, and then rises up to Saltway Farm on the left.

Turn left onto a farm track here and continue walking for some little while until you come to some farm buildings at a point where you are directed in no uncertain terms, by means of another yellow arrow, to bear right alongside some woodland. The track will take you down towards still more farm buildings, curve left past them, and then right, and debouch at a road opposite some large barns. Bear left here, and head towards the house you see ahead. Cross the road and you will descend a pretty street lined with cottages, which is the typical Cotswold hamlet of Calcot.

Immediately after the last house on the left is a gate. Pass through this into a meadow and head for a stile in front of you at the edge of some woods. Cross the stile and turn right to follow the path until it meets the river. Keep going as you approach a house of mansion proportions but do not enter the grounds. Walk alongside the river until you come to a bridge opposite the house at a point where the river loops around an island.

Cross the bridge and follow the path as it bears right and heads in the direction of the village and church, passing a highly attractive garden on the left. The entrance to the church is another path on the right. One can do no better than quote the history of the church (available for purchase within): " to light upon a Saxon building, retaining its original ground plan, together with examples of long-and-short-work, pilaster strips, a window, and a chancel arch, besides other pre-Norman features , to find all this, and then to realise that no single authoritative allusion has been made to it in the county literature...is nothing short of amazing".

After visiting the church return to the main path, turn right, and then left at the road. Keep going until you come to the point where the walk began.

The COLN ROGERS Walk

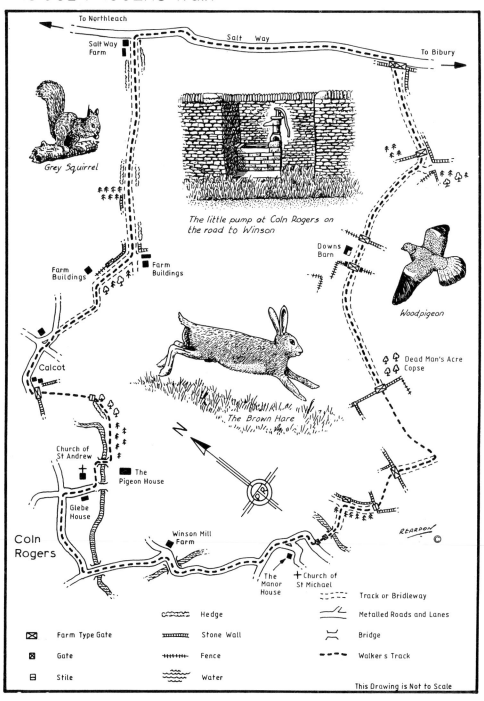

To Northleach

Salt Way

To Bibury

Salt Way Farm

Grey Squirrel

The little pump at Coln Rogers on the road to Winson

Downs Barn

Farm Buildings

Farm Buildings

Woodpigeon

Calcot

Dead Man's Acre Copse

The Brown Hare

Church of St Andrew

The Pigeon House

Glebe House

Coln Rogers

Winson Mill Farm

The Manor House

Church of St Michael

REARDON ©

		Track or Bridleway
⊠ Farm Type Gate	⌒⌒⌒ Hedge	⊃⊂ Metalled Roads and Lanes
⊠ Gate	⊞⊞⊞ Stone Wall	⌒⌒ Bridge
⊟ Stile	+++ Fence	− − − Walkers Track
	∿∿∿ Water	

This Drawing is Not to Scale

10. Apperley/Deerhurst

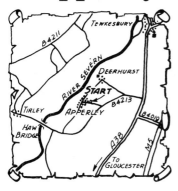

Distance: 5 miles

Time: 2hrs continuous walking

Map: OS Pathfinder SO 82/92, Cheltenham

Starting Point: Grid ref 863285

Terrain: Generally flat, through grassy meadows and along metalled lanes.

Refreshments: Two pubs en route - the Coal House at Apperley and the New Inn at Haw Bridge. There is also a village shop in Apperley.

THIS walk is almost completely flat with only the merest hint of a slope. It runs through meadows on the banks of England's greatest river and along lanes through charming villages to one of the oldest chapels in the country. There is one small regret: at one stage the walk takes you along a major road for about 10 minutes (although there is a means of avoiding it). This is the perfect walk for a drowsy summer's day - or after one Yorkshire pudding too many....

The walk begins in the centre of Apperley, at the crossroads near to the timbered village shop and post office. Park where you can and stroll down the road signposted for Tewkesbury and Cheltenham and the village hall. You will pass a selection of mostly new houses, then a road named Apperley Park on the left, then an older white cottage across the road to the right. Yet more houses of recent vintage appear to the left, followed by an old timbered cottage. The road curves slightly to the right and then, right at the very edge of the village, is the entrance to the village hall on the left.

Go into the hall grounds and cross the car park. Once you are on the grass head for a stile which is just visible to the left of the far goal post. You will find, in fact, that the stile is the first of two separated by a little wooden bridge. Hop over these into a cultivated field across which is an obvious path that cuts its way to another 'V' shaped stile. This brings you into a meadow.

The path is not so obvious here but by keeping to the hedge on the right hand side you cannot go wrong. Very soon you will come to a mound on the right that conceals a pond. Follow, bearing right, the curve of the mound and of the field until you see a gate set into the far right hand corner across the field. Already there are marvellous views to the slopes beyond, particularly when they are painted with brilliant yellow oil-seed rape.

Next to the gate is a stile which you should cross to bring you onto a metalled lane. Admire the view across the fields to the church spire, still more beautiful from here, before passing through another metal gate to your right. This takes you into a field, most of which is to be under cultivation. You, however, need only approach the edge of it before turning left across the rough patch in the corner towards a well concealed stile in the hedgerow about 25 or 30 yards to the right of the gate you have just come through.

On the other side of the stile is a sloping field. Beyond is the tower of Deerhurst Church with, to the left, a timbered house adjoining a stone construction, Odda's Chapel, which you will be passing later. Go over the brow of the hill towards a brick house on the left.

Just to the right of the house is a stile. Surmount this (or pass under the barbed wire next to it) and head diagonally left across the field before you, roughly in the direction of the thatched timbered cottage ahead of you. The stile you want is in the hedgerow to the left, just after the second of two stumpy trees. Once over the stile you will find yourself in a road where you should turn right. After about 50 yards you will pass a gate on the right and then a concrete buttress on the left with wooden railings. Step up to this and enter what seems to be a garden. It is, but the right of way skirts the garden in the long grass to the left and fetches you up to a stile that leads into a meadow. Beyond the meadow is Odda's Chapel.

Walk along the spine of the mound in front of you and then cut diagonally across the meadow to the right, towards the chapel, until you come to a stile just to the left of it. Pass through this to find yourself in front of a gate. Eventually you will resume the walk by going through the gate and heading towards the river but in the meantime you may like to visit Odda's Chapel to the right and even the Parish Church which is a couple of hundred yards farther on. The chapel is delightful - it is late-Saxon, built by Odda, a kinsman of King Edward the Confessor, in memory of his brother Elfric and dedicated in 1056. The chapel later became part of the priory which gave rise to the quaint proximity of the farmhouse.

The church, further along the road, is worth a visit too. Deerhurst ('the forest of wild animals') was once an important place, site of the chief monastery of the Saxon kingdom of Hwicce. Here Canute and Edmund Ironside signed the treaty that divided England between Saxon and Dane. By the 10th Century the monastery was no longer pre-eminent, although an Archbishop of Canterbury, Alphege, was a monk here. Edward the Confessor made it a cell of St Denis in Paris and in 1440 its lands were given to Eton College. After the Dissolution of the Monasteries the monastery church became the parish church, one of the finest Saxon churches in the country. Of particular note is the tower, much of which dates back to the late-Saxon period, the superb Saxon front, the finest in existence, and, outside on the old apse, the ninth century Saxon carving known as the Deerhurst Angel. A booklet giving more details about the church is available in the church itself at a reasonable price.

After visiting the chapel and church you continue the walk by passing through the gate near the chapel and walking along the track until the River Severn appears in front of you. At a spreading oak tree turn left onto the Severn Way.

It is impossible to go wrong, really. With the river on your right the path is pretty obvious, usually some 20 yards in from the river bank, often on a raised mound. Soon you will come to a stile - cross this with the boat club to the right on the opposite bank and enter a meadow where a group of holding pens are scattered among the flowers. Another stile (with 'no elvering' sign) takes you into a narrower path in the grip of the river and trees. The path narrows further to bring you into a sort of orchard area passing a red-roofed shed and then a house, behind which is a sizeable pond. Then the path opens up to a meadow once again and the path will deliver you over a stile into the welcome portals of the Coal House Inn, where a good beer may be enjoyed and where the landlord will undoubtedly water your panting dog.

Now you have a choice. For those who wish to avoid the walk on the main road it is possible to take a short cut back to Apperley. Walk out of the pub and take the road behind it until you see a track and cattle grid on your right. Across the field to the right of the track

ODDA'S CHAPEL AT DEERHURST

is a gate and a stile. By crossing this and walking directly up the hill to another stile and continuing over the brow you will arrive in Apperley.

For walkers wishing to extend their stroll, you will find a path just to the left of the gate into the caravan park. Pass through the park until after about 50 yards you meet a stile. Cross this into a meadow and keep to the obvious path as it follows the course of the river. The scene has a gentle rustic beauty appropriate to a bucolic poem. After about 300 yards you will come to another stile, which you take, as the river veers away to the right. The path recovers the course of the river and heads for a bridge, with a pub, the New Inn, to its right. Pass through a gate to the left of Haw Bridge and turn left onto the road.

The road is fairly busy and there is no consistent path. Keep going for about half a mile until you come to a large lay-by on the left, opposite a lane signposted for Wainlode and Norton. The lay-by is overhung by trees that almost conceal a white fence with a gate. Go through this into the woods and follow the path as it meanders through thick undergrowth. The path slopes gently up and emerges on to a lane with a large white residence, Apperley House, on the right, surrounded by garden and lawn. Behind you to the right you can glimpse views towards the Vale of Gloucester and the hills beyond.

Continue along the lane as it passes through a metal gate. Soon you will see a white, timbered cottage in front of you across the fields to the right and then another similar one suddenly appears on the left beside the road. Soon the lane passes through another gate and passes Holy Trinity church on the right, whose belfry is surmounted, curiously, by a fish. Beyond is the village pond and the war memorial. Between them is a tree planted in 1977 to commemorate the silver jubilee of Queen Elizabeth II. At this point the lane meets a road. Bear left onto this and follow it as it passes some delightful houses back to the centre of Apperley.

The APPERLEY-DEERHURST Walk

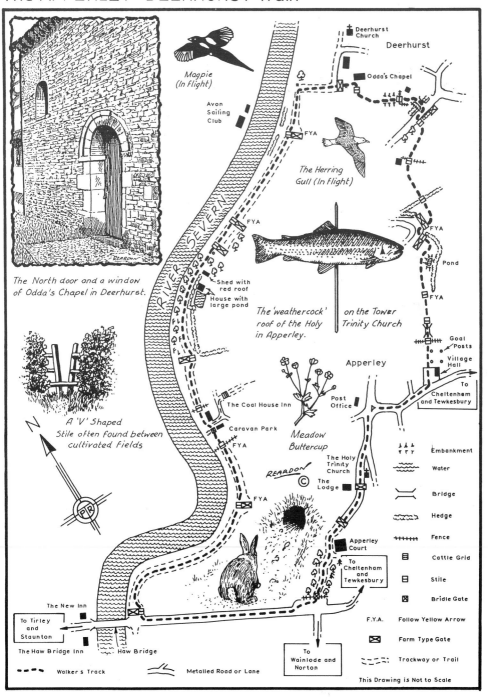

The North door and a window of Odda's Chapel in Deerhurst.

A 'V' Shaped Stile often found between cultivated fields

Magpie (In Flight)

Avon Sailing Club

The Herring Gull (In flight)

Deerhurst Church

Deerhurst

Odda's Chapel

FYA

FYA

Pond

FYA

FYA

Goal Posts

Village Hall

To Cheltenham and Tewkesbury

Shed with red roof

House with large pond

The 'weathercock' on the Tower roof of the Holy Trinity Church in Apperley.

Apperley

Post Office

The Coal House Inn

Caravan Park

FYA

Meadow Buttercup

The Holy Trinity Church

The Lodge

FYA

REARDON ©

Apperley Court

To Cheltenham and Tewkesbury

The New Inn

To Tirley and Staunton

The Haw Bridge Inn   Haw Bridge

To Wainlode and Norton

RIVER SEVERN

N

REARDON

▲▲▲ / ▼▼▼	Embankment
〜〜〜	Water
⌣⌢	Bridge
〰〰	Hedge
+++++	Fence
⊟	Cattle Grid
⊟	Stile
⊠	Bridle Gate
F.Y.A.	Follow Yellow Arrow
⊠	Farm Type Gate
⌐ ⌐ ⌐	Trackway or Trail

This Drawing is Not to Scale

- - -   Walker's Track   〜〜   Metalled Road or Lane

43

REARDON PUBLISHING
A family run publishing house based in Cheltenham, producing guides to the Cotswold area, using local authors, and having the books printed in Gloucestershire/Cotswolds.

Other books in the Walkabout series

COTSWOLD WALKABOUT   by N. REARDON
0 950867 40 3

GLOUCESTERSHIRE WALKABOUT   by N. REARDON
0 950867 49 7

COTSWOLD HILLWALKS   by C. KNOWLES
0 950867 45 4

The Echo's COTSWOLD WALKS   by C. KNOWLES
1 873877 03 X

The Echo's second book of
COTSWOLD WALKS   by C. KNOWLES
1 873877 04 8

THE DONNINGTON WAY   by C. HANDY
1 874192 00 6

COTSWOLD RIVERWALKS   by C. HANDY
1 873877 05 6

WALKS AROUND STOW-ON-THE-WOLD   by M. RICHARDS
0 950867 48 9

WALKS AROUND GREAT TEW
and THE ROLLRIGHT STONES   by M. RICHARDS
1 873877 02 1

WALKS AROUND CHIPPING NORTON   by M. RICHARDS
1 873877 01 3

Please send a S.A.E. for our free Booklist and Orderform
To: **REARDON PUBLISHING, 56, UPPER NORWOOD STREET, LECKHAMPTON, CHELTENHAM, GLOS. GL53 0DU**